MONETIZED

ALISSA QUART

MONETIZED

MIAMI UNIVERSITY PRESS

LIBRARY OF CONGRESS
CATALOGING-IN-PUBLICATION DATA
QUART, ALISSA.
[POEMS. SELECTIONS]
MONETIZED / BY ALISSA QUART.
PAGES CM
ISBN 978-1-881163-56-5
I. TITLE.
PS3617.U367A6 2015
811'.6—DC23

COVER PHOTOGRAPH: MARILYN MINTER,
SPYDER, 2005. C PRINT. COURTESY OF
THE ARTIST, SALON 94, NEW YORK
AND REGEN PROJECTS, LOS ANGELES

PRINTED ON ACID-FREE, RECYCLED PAPER
IN THE UNITED STATES OF AMERICA

MIAMI UNIVERSITY PRESS
356 BACHELOR HALL
MIAMI UNIVERSITY
OXFORD, OHIO 45056

AS ALWAYS, THIS BOOK IS DEDICATED TO
PETER MAASS AND CLEO QUART MAASS.

I

II

III

I

DRIFTWOOD

One day you are ordering extra
olives and the next day, one
of The Damned.

I had worked this carapace
that I lived in: modular, notched,
pieces of oak. I built myself
of driftwood, cables.
My face forced yet nonchalant.
Sometimes I was an artist's
wife, my dress long, hair
a sheaf. Sometimes
I was an extra on *Cop Rock*.
A singing policewoman
waiting for crimes
to be committed.

Sometimes I prevailed:
a memo, lithographic,
afternoon-like, sharp-edged.

The stamp of unbelonging
had always belonged to me.

Soon I returned to anywhere
but the beginning.
Homes of cockroaches.
Sunken rooms of bruisers.
Islands of police Sirens.
Each year was broken
back into pieces

of driftwood, as if born
to lose. An explosive device
in every pot.

EXPRESS

Amtrak diaspora
you listen to a song
"1985" as you couldn't
listen to the year itself.
That's a word-slash-thing
and a right-now-nostalgia–
thing. You read the factory
of human fate is the novel.
So we are all small store
owners getting self-help
goods from these factories.

A train: a series
of moving corridors.
Sleeping addict's family
with cookie-tins-as-toys;
old woman putting burned
CDs in cases, thinks
she's still working.
Papers in a business
man's accordion

folder dropping to collages
of aspiration. White
rectangles on a train floor.

Every moving window, bridge,
snow, farm silo, is a harbinger.
Sign for *Felt Shoes*.
Snowplow lemon
yellow, gravel,
I still exist, a tarp.

MAGNETIC RESONANCE

Within the magnetic life-
sized hold, all sounds,
all pictures, are stooges.
Clang of deprivation, buzz
of sense. Sounding mistakes.
The best one: allowing
youth to end.

They give you a check-
list of American self-
destruction. Does your body
have shrapnel? Tattoos
meant to change your life?
A nose pierce? The false hip,
the metal knee—arrows.
Pinned elbows: *sportif*
wands. The breast implant
meant to make him love you.
Or, yes, god knows, the penile,
the metal, stone, mass, rip, tear.
If your ring is real, it won't
hurt. If it aches, you'll know

how little he spent
to make you his robot,
his Saint Sebastian. Iron
chains whine loose,
ferries in black water
thump their metal
crossings to some-
where darker, a forgotten
night club, a subway's
halting sparks.
Stranger music.

THIEF

His chest hair: a nest.
His lady: a vanity
mirror. James Caan
and Tuesday Weld start
over in each scene
as The Method taught.

His face a drill
bit. He's a Lincoln
convertible. He's unconverted.
An industrial park kick-
back, pinky ring.
That's all mod con-ned.
A Buddhist burglar.
That's the coolest Jew.

She's vanilla, genital, secretarial.
Rabbit fur cashier.
Dangling passivity;
masochism expert.
A purloined bride packs

female heat like lambskin rugs,
thick cotton skirts.
"I'm your woman!" she sobs.

"Let's get on with the story and get
married," says he in a diner on top
of Chicago sludge.
The Elevated shaking
the salt and pepper.

Together, they are white flight.

■

He breaks a bank vault;
thievery also labor.

Tuesday eggs him on with breasts
like Friday, eyes like Sunday, bottle
blonde of Wednesday. The hand-
cuff earrings of Monday.

He survives her and the mob, explodes
our bars and our houses.
Cue fiery baptism.

Jews kill people, too, through
our toughest actors.
Adam, Moses.

■

For the rest of us, starting anew,
another vehicle for shame.

We could forgive ourselves
if only we knew our own story.
Our fracture our annealing.

Are we starting again or reentering
the life, of heists, bar
brawls and bullet pocks? *As if*
for the first time.

Suburban lawns
part beneath our feet.

MY OWN PRIVATE IDAHO

Identity politics' age
of innocence. Track-marked
novelists slumbered, their hair
flopped, their shirts autumnal,
all the color of rocks, cavorting
like field mice. Leaving burning
houses in Tulsa or ashen
trailer parks in Oregon.
How long could it go on
before the designer
drug deaths of the Shakespearean
surfers? Phoenixes on
the carrion of their brother's
slacker longueur: Mala
Noche now a nightclub.

We were a short
story of better
commerce, a human
collage of natural
cigarettes, Budapest

hickeys, cool
hunting manuals.
Dirtsploitation.
The fucked up face
of the landscape was ours.

STRIP

I am walking on the median:
Mother liked the words "bird feeder";
she said, "Well-loved boys
look alike." This truism sold
on the street. Boys vended like
knock-off musks.

On the median, I wear orange
silk shirts, a lady reporter
drinking rainbow cocktails
with Liebling. Call it
"the manic defense" or "high style."
Eros or its opposite. Standing
between well-loved
and unloved versions of "to be."

Wear an orange shirt like a life raft
on the median. You say, "A real thief
would steal your heartbeat."
I say, "Childhood is said to be 'rich'
because we visit it so often."

HOLIDAY

Overcame the year of choice
through tragedy's single outcome.
Dank gray carpet nubs, heroin
chic rictus. Hid in the revival
house. Covered misgivings
with theatrical paint.
As Ann Harding said in *Holiday*:
"When there's smoke there's usually
someone smoking." The panoramic
mirror of '94 was antic, Depression-
era. Boffins wore checkered
jackets. Men had overcoats inside
their bodies. Spoke
in American actor British.

Always imitating, I wore
thin frocks to escape.
Post-partisan nervosa.
My immigrant students learned
American confessions. Radical
prof told me incorrect English
renewed language.

Scottish deaf woman lip-
read only dialect. Corrected
my social class through
Anglican boyfriends insisting
they were aliens.

"Can I go home now?" I asked
book covers. Tried to tell
captivity stories without breaking
out. Dittos for class-
room use. Youth made me
a cut-away shot, a thing
on loan. Like library
books in resort
towns. "Anything done well is
an imitation," the Buddhist
poet told me, his malignant
tongue cut out. Around us,
folded paper obits, dried
hydrangeas, Modernist poets
finishing their dying.

We were parlor
room comedies, exploded
from the inside. Gauze

dresses, typed copies.
Who was grading?
The answer key buried
in the second act's
potted palm.
If we do this well,
it is an imitation.

ANOTHER TEEN MOVIE

Skanky girls scream to their eyeliner,
create aquarium atmo.
The boy cruises Corollas. Old men
crown him a Matt Dillon poster.
A puppy love trickster.
The young hero then strips
to the waist. Floats down the river,
underdressed. He swims in
dun lust. Reminds us
that teens on film
reflect adult prohibition.
This boy is a rumble fish,
his own authorship firked out.
Seems free but is trapped
like the filmgoer, stuck in
a murky lozenge of a scene
until fadeout.

EPITHALAMIUM

For Josh and Devorah

An ancient wedding
vase. Unseen figures
in the procession scene
are, of course, the gods.
You're Eros & Co.
You're a modest garden
that's a feverish park.
You're sedition, plot.
In this comedy, you are
displaced. You know
this well: you face
the face.

Our juvie dreadlocks, our trendy
Euro wedlock. Once, we walked
all day. Held our Smarties
high by ponds; shambled
in procession; smoked
until we fell asleep.

The pressure to be clever
yet no math for tracing
our imperium.

On antique vases, we're frankly
nude. West Hollywood, Attic, belated,
classical, available.
Our lack made us
become ourselves.

Wedding: an entrance.
To entrance: to enter,
to be hypnotized.

Our hidden leaders
have burning torches.
Our visible heroes
will take us
round. Always, all
love is clay.
You'll be yourselves
yet also procession.
Eros will hold your veil.
You are the faces
facing the Other.

ZENITH

Household objects told
their story best. Danish
walnut center-
piece. Barrettes
never said her name.
Metal-armed
lamps. Tropicana
in units. The parka
he never buttoned.
Bank giveaways: the Zenith,
black-and-white, fritzing.
Standstill also utopia.
Hitting that TV
it came alive.
Sparked back up.
That it might show another life.
That it might show them life.

GIRLS I HAVE LOVED

1.

R. snickers when I say I listen to public radio. Radio should be private, as in the song "Private Eyes" or a secreted social intelligence. New York exhales recession. I am ten. R. is 11 and not rich though she lives over a garden. Her family eats spaghetti often and she glamorizes her bunk bed. The acne on the sides of her nose enchant, two twin flags of adolescence, the miserable mount awaiting me. With extremely combed hair, luncheon foods wrapped in plastic, and old lady good handwriting, R. will win some prize, I think. She tells me to buy Best of Records. I give us code names after spices. R. is Hot Pepper. I am Cinnamon: placating, invisible. The grown-ups' jacket pins announce their subjectivities. They are small parts of the death of punk. I write reports on the rainforest. I would like to live there. God is George Washington on the front of the quarter.

2.

At twelve, T. looks like a horse but is too tasteful to be a horse girl. She has the long fingers of a pianist. She does not have the temperament of one who practices. Tall and smart looking, she is not sixth-grade pretty. She is practicing for when she will be the living sign of young sex, in three years, impressively wry about boobs and tatas. She smokes downstairs. I don't know where that is. She never does anything bad for the first time, has always done it already. I wonder about the latchkey kid cosmopolites, the ones who don't bunt their softballs. What do they do when they are alone? What does everybody do all day and what do they talk about? After all, secondary sex characteristics only appear to me when I look them up in the *Women's Health Manual*. My favorite dirty word is abortion.

3.

A pugilistic blonde, C. affects a half-hearted rejection of the New York rich girls who have always embraced her. "What's your gambit?" she says. I am nineteen. Her pale-haired head and her skirt shimmer. Her self-conviction is bottomless. I learn from C. the inches permissible during the return of the flair jean—three. The proper coding for melancholia—a Neapolitan silent screen star crying. A dinner—four spoons of tahini in front of a 1960's photo of Cuba. Generic cigarettes—proud poverty. The Good—marginal parents. Knowledge—to be worn lightly but constantly cited, and never finding its expression in the Law. Beauty—ostensibly invisible but always in use like drugs.

4.

Then there's diminutive, ductile, duplicitous Z., spoiled, bat mitz-
vah girl for the ages F., everyone-thinks-I-am-beautiful I., tall im-
posing sophistic E., exacting, cruel motherly L., shining, willfully
complacent, star-mad J., shaky lyrical suicide-to-be P.

5.

Girls I have loved cover their eyes with fine shiny hair, tug on their
small ears and wraith-like wrists, emanate throaty laughs, heal oc-
casional infections, powder over their impoverishments. Every
dyad is a chance for them to deploy their own romance. They are
vicious protectors with rice papery skin, slang-slingers, evaders,
wise-asses, nice people. I am leaving out the girls I have left.

RED RIDING TRILOGY

Horror films are
sometimes memoirs.
In this one, the usual,
inquiry killed. Small
children went dead.
Moors wasted. A house,
a human abattoir.
Pervy with pen
knives. Florid pub
wallpaper, a carpet
where viewers pattern
their own ill-
spent hours. Yorkshire,
outlandish and sad,
like Florida. Entertainment,
a murder, too.
Of time. Memoirs are
also home devices.
Audiences victims, too.
Leave your London
house, now, your youth
spent by others.

Manky street fellows
follow, to phone booths.
Point at *The Sun*'s jugs.
Hold your dusty
thistles, feet in Mary
Janes, hands on dense
lace curtains. Your hot
water bottle your lousy
midnight protector.
Somewhere, the P.M.
clutches her purse,
between poll
taxes; someone chains
themselves to a power
plant. If horror
films are memoirs we
must be aware
early. And memoirs
are always home
devices. Diversion
a weapon.

PROMISSORY

By an improved anguish . . .
—LAURA RIDING

The rich have desire, a balsam
and marzipan habitus. We others
have only need. His cheques

tore a hole, invented
the right track
lighting, initiated adult
programming, regulated weather,
turned the sky to a blue chemise.

The legumes rioted though,
burnt themselves in the pan.
Affianced, their financials got weak.
Cable never arrived
anywhere. Bank holiday turned
to a snow bank. He insisted
he be the analgesic
of common sense, she be
children's chewables.
At all those third parties

girls closed, men waited
to insert themselves.
This twosome a third term,
watching the parlor
aspirants swallow salary.
He responded he was not
a third person. She said together
they might fissure
the scenarist's false
blizzard. Continuing
education should end, he said.

The floors and windows grew
so nice that while they could
slate and pine, a human
might never live there.

QUALIA BEFORE BEDTIME

A man can be what we want
yet still not what we choose.
A decahedron on blackboard
facing. A pedagogical
erasure that ties, hectors,
inserts itself, reminds that it
doesn't care, and then,
"Didn't you feel it
this time, if not
the others?" That's metro-
instrumentalism or
sleazy mentalism.
Throwing care
at the shadow stiff
then swallowing whatever
stray elements
come. With all the notes
struck minor key, and
for, truly, a mirror's
audience. And still
throwing care for
care is what we make

movies about, what
we invented the theremin for.
Qualia before bedtime.

Where else might we go to settle
ourselves inside other selves? Fit
the girls in the white cotton
dress inside the girls in the dark
dress? Array a number of painted
faces; control violent borders;
enter, lashes curled for masquerade.
Blink, and go on.

THE TERMS

Middle-aged men make good bad mothers.

People are just show tunes looking for a show.

The word "classic" accompanies the word "commercial," after
1943.

Writers are still worrying about the word not meeting the thing it
describes. Who else cares.

Even yoked beasts have private thoughts.

All thoughts are interruptions.

II

SPRING BREAKS

This beach, an old
song. Hunters look
for fortunes under sandy Buds,
days are day-glo,
cars are topless.
See your face
in the mirrored yacht floor?
Dipsomaniac mothers mouth
"Ring my bell," injured,
on the shore, sands holding
our armpit skull tattoos,
rocking little bods, our shaved
chest zoo, as poolside aging
cling to dwindling heat.
Our kids' thick flesh
pelts twice our size.
All our sport
shirts point to always
sitting still. Particles:
fried, bored, alive.

Can we refuse ourselves?
Millennial bland angels
tech-tonically tapping, our sweat-
free abalone blouses,
signatured water?
Neon-hearted: let us be
shielded. Here, where
the naughts end,
unnoticed, where yachts
hope shiningly unbought.
All owners at risk. All trying
to float. This beach's
undimpled flesh exists
for death cult ex-marines,
for illustrated boyfriends,
for ruin. It's waiting for
something to rise
again. You will only
reproduce your life.

VIEWS

Anorectic transplant flashes
skin at fashion sisters.
Liquid Paper arms.
Vanishing: an aesthetic.
Home is a lead-painted hut.
An occupational art
therapist made luxury
cubes. She photo shopped.
A liberal arts stripper
silver collared herself,
souvenir to man's bad taste.

"Crush" is a verb here,
noun inside waits.
Vintage blouses offer
reprisal. A mile more
this retro plane passes
into unfinished pastness.

These are the lower middle's
unlovely places, all named

as paradises: Sunset
Park, Neptune Avenue, Mid-
wood. Elm-shaded mother-

daughter houses. Managerial
class fear of falling. Serge-
suited, a strollered citizen's
brigade. *Saturday Evening
Post*-its. They do not notice

a man's tattooed torso,
an ice cream cake falling
into mortification
as ceremony turns mourning
to nostalgia and villains
and cities go on.

SOLARIZED

Our serrated landscape
full of digits.
Dial, keloid, data.

If trees are still "in"
we can thumb
through not click-through.

Books are so over
though. All those chyrons
for The End. Tomorrow's

programming is surely lethal.
We are hanging on by a high
thread count, glass

stemware of the old regime.
A room of Vrooms.
Let's hope we're perennial.
We are woodcuts.
Ramulose as a lending library.

City trees still obscure teens,
futons and jack-offs. Shade
the elderly and their fusilli.
Can we join them?

Children steal adults' adulthood.
Adults steal one another.

PALM SPRINGS AT
THE END OF THE MIND

A father counted cards,
his prized club sandwiches
small wagers from aged
sports gods. Bain de
Soleil the height of local
vocabulary. Slim-
Fast sped time.
So did valets, fondues,
tan-thighed gals with
department store names.
Eyes matched the pool.

Then time shrank. Paid
gossips and hard rulers
of state drifted off
to eras where their names
were blanks. Stiff
Halstons withered.
Pools turned cold,
chlorine flecked green,

mold dusted gruyère.
A Hollywood no
longer in syndication.

I'd like to say solidarity
would have helped them.
But who really knows?
And what came next?
Many later fatherlands
we fixed upon
that always failed us.

MANHUNTER

Her white blond child runs in the supermarket
Bisquick, loves the baddie, not his Mother
of the Latchkeys. Men with missions
dial white phones with fervor.
Hotel rooms arrive by lighted elevators.
Well-heeled blood. Beige wife
riffles affluence. Frankenstein and the G-man
dirty dance. Audience plays
the fire, missing prints on toilet
tissue, murderer's stain. We inflame
the Steppenwolf-fetching thesp to choke
a Hollywood reporter. The film believes
language is waste, is a prison. That the audience
is a bullet failing to lodge in
a detective's skull. Enlightened
refuse, we already know the monster.
Detective capers communicate like hospitals,
serving the outlying areas.

THE GLOW OF IT

Lurch under branches flocked
by killer ice. The past's not there.
Time's arrows don't point
round, upwards or fall.
We go straight then dash.
A woman's red hair lighting
the wall means nothing
after all. There will
be no nature, just a second
set of blinds. Behind us:
night sky of black construction
paper. Our instructions? Pass on
our heartbeats. Become lap-
top holds of amber cells.
Flame out, drawn in.
Screened then quartered.
Raging for duplication
yet little moving us anymore.

DRIVES

These drives: a child beaten
poolside. Stones as spy
signs. Girls moving their heads
when they want you
to disappear. A red-faced father.
Stiff-backed trickster.
A boy crying in his sleep.
A code breaker doing math
in his head. There are new fruits,
larger denominations.
You learn to hide cell phones
explicitly, to talk percents.
To be thick with legal.

You'd no permit before so
you never got caught
speeding or picked up
younger sisters after
work or had a trunk,
or a gallon or sour
mix or mixed
tapes that you played

on the Interstate.
Never got the hell out
of that town.

The first boys had greasy
shadows, moving in tandem
with their Camrys.
Drove for fries, to hide,
get high, self-immolate.
Soon, their driving
became clean drinking
glasses, calamine
lotion, buried
sadness, cybersmog.
Towns Canaan,
Goshen, Queechy.
Finally possessing
locating systems in
the dark, as if
America was theirs.

FOSTERING

Our coterie adopts
ideas and positions;
births a single child
of great science; talks
heads and fosters opinion.

But what of the true
biological wax? Mussed
cat hair; hurled clay
containers; not-ginned-
up feeling; the chat show
host who asks, "What's
a broken heart?"

That guy writes theme books,
shared white jeans with a Beatle's
son. His repeated nightmare:
he's the unknown
Green Room guest
bumped off
the program.

PROTOCOL

We can't forget our time.
Such forgetting is an error
of sense. Forget an age
of shoe bomber, of underwear
detonator, of airplane
null. Forget American
Gosselin serialism: eight
children they do not
love; a dozen screens,
playing losing games.
These are all signs; bright
as a street corner,
audible as punks-with-beasts.

New York's dowdy
towers, sentinels.
A time unmarked,
unremarkable. Save for
the rise of protocol.

AGE OF ANXIETY REDUX

Maine: "The way life should be."
Genetic material in the quilted
corners of B & B's.
"How Soon Is Now" raining down
near a "canine rest area,"
then a "game weighing station."
The bucks are always versus does.
We are Minerva but the boys
think our robes are bed sheets
to get under. We are aloft
and not a loft bed, a colossus
and not its wreath.
We must believe our own desire
more than their desire to own.

A flag equals a state of comfort.
Your hair soft from forty
years of conditioning. We cruise
through naughty forests soon-to-be
pine-scented stationery;
by miles-long logging trains
then passages cleared by log-rolling.

Spy the lobster broth-drinkers,
the whale-bottomed political dynasties,
the obese weekenders coddling
eggs optimistically with the sea,
the Brahmin disowning
himself on Marginal Way.

We'll deposit fur and tears,
spermatozoa of meme,
in the corners of rented rooms
as the coastal cities slide
on their axes, looking
to find their correction.

THE 51ST STATE

Hold back the edges of your gowns,
Ladies, we are going through hell.
—WILLIAM CARLOS WILLIAMS

Deep sea swim in post-
feminist two-piece.
Your white limbs disarticulate.
Sea cucumbers, floating,
filling the joint.

In the too concrete hotel
eco-tourists come and go.
We're netted:
you serve yourself just
enough for the French press,
not enough to go
around. Explosively,
inattentively premarital.

Near the seashell Pac Men
Gringo Lebowskis watch Texan
teens kayak under parrot

canopies. As if
this land was their land.
Water goes dark.

O dry adulthood!
On the other side of this
island of vows there will be
vined mysteries. There will be old
age. Like science fiction.
Could it really happen here?
It will, as marriage is a mangrove
of loss, us two, a tourist
revenge tragedy, the Blue
Beach given to the hotel
chain, I'm given to you.

EXPECTED

They promised this would make you better, natural, without fumes or lead. You were closed before but after you might *be here now*. Go into the future as you could not be in the past.

Gestation: an emergency registered as expected.

A natural emergency followed by other ones like it. Your instructions: absorb the newcomer.

A fetus conjures synesthesia.

Beach, street, and offices. They stink. Cabbages are infants' heads; passing faces the green of cucumbers; surfaces are vents.

All for a newborn tyrant. She will arrive and wear the tiniest lemon pants, the smallest sage hat. Cotton crowned and romper-ed. Sleeper-ed. Wiped and footed.

These will be acts of faith. Making you now a site to be believed.

As if you are a house. Improperly bolted, proofed and attached. Yet still expecting the new visitor.

MESMERISM

The American flag by Jasper Johns and then by George
W. A wheel, a plate, a spindle, a salted glass.

Incomplete forms held us most: hypnosis of the half-
circle, of matrix and failed immanence.
Why we dreamt of those we'd broken with yet
not ones we really loved.
Low and high times:
incomplete, unfinished. Canyons
at the end of our minds.

TIME OUT

Here, where they cancelled
out the saint's eyes,
his face cut, rendered
aporia. How we replace our
selves: decapitate an image.

■

To banish dictator or martyr,
a brush, knife or axe.

Another designated
savior, illustrated to fill
his place, gold wash, neutral beige
of fifteenth century, conceals

our faith with other faith.
But nothing is ever
void.

■

Hagia Sophia. So ill-
preserved. A wobbly
argument for ruin-as-
beauty, a rotted lace
near the throat of the dead.

Every mosaic, torsos
painted over, metaphoric gouge
where eye should be.

Time condensed is human
force: iconoclasm,
the ultimate condensation.

How we replace ourselves.

INSTRUMENTAL

There, reading against the traffic, a car
crash between chapters.

Alphabet via street
signs: C is for Con Ed.

Kids' music
meant an actual kid, singing to herself past
the silent billboards.

■

Then those days—when you were starting out,
as they say—you were sulfur

frozen at The Odeon
when strapped to the masthead,
every remark, aside,
sharpened.

The table by the mirror reserved
for all the baby lionesses.

And now. You are living the app.
A pop-up. La Vida App!

■

An instrument of life,
of instrumental life.
In those days—raised by the book, zine,
velveteen couch. African
violet. Your face in the spider
plants. *World of Our Fathers*, Serpico edition.

Hairy men bearing
Bronx–Yonkers vowels.
Famous daughters' names
hidden, like classical music in restaurants.

Children hide under oak tables.
Everyone under nine is "Outta sight!"

■

All stars, all likes. All nothing.

And you know, it's so much like every culture

business in which you are really nothing,
with some handler/mother/father guiding you along
toward option or percent or foreign.

You are something waiting to be nothing or vice
versa. As value is circulation.

The Twitter Dead Souls told me.

■

Ann says in Minnesota it was
peer therapy on the phone or over coffee
or on plush ottomans.

You'd talk for an hour then
the peer for her hour.

Unlike a real friendship, so to speak,
each person had to listen

their allotted time.

Now, the ads talk to us all
in cars. Bus stops move with

product. Streaming, advertorial, posted, scraped,
mined. Reading is fracking.

BabywithiPad.jpg
Friends are what we handle.

Too many words,
not enough ears.

LEAVING OUT

I am second generation to the second,
tired of carrying more than the others.

Sometimes I manage the scenic route:
Early Milk-Fed, Late Corn-Fed.

Splitsville whirrs us back to ontology.

"What's the point?" seeps out
of that hyperlink.

My seaweed anklet is farewell's
metonym. Jewel root surrounds
poison ivy. Like love, salve
grows round bane.

GREEN FAIRY

after Andrew Lang's Fairy Books

Poke for blood 2 x
a day. How sugary

is it. The unborn filters
sweets, steals bones,

peels teeth, dines
on fingernails.

So a breakfast must be
eaten, hands sanitized. Lancets

bright plastic. Bloody pricks
should protect us. Nausea

physical then metaphysical.
Opposite of philosophical

upset cured by pregnancy.
Cioran wrote that thoughts

derive from thwarted sensations.
Where's the sweet lacquer

around me, the Necco candy
mother's coating I'd been

promised? This maternity oxidizes
on contact: acrid, residual.

Silver polish. But mothers should be
base not acid. Make cowls, salve.

Fairy books warned of cruel queens.
A line of mothers, hands lanced.

CLEAN

Searches on the engine equal
human thoughts, key
strokes stand-ins for
inner life. They left him

with Chekhov. Key to the Russian
character. Oligarchs wanting
Snowden for dinner parties.

To this we say:
clean install.
A further encryption
fends off brute force.

We'll only know who we are
once the algorithm
finds us.
Data at rest
of equal danger
as data moving.

STRONG COPIES

A mind interrupted is still a mind.

Here's to reproduction: photography, Twitter, pregnancy.

Women may mother in order to be loved.

Some only wish for another adult's love.

That t-shirt reads America's Next Top Bottom.

Absolute powerlessness corrupts absolutely.

Envy the young boys still close to being children.

The older men will always be their own children.

WOMANIZED

Late marriage and late Modernism:
both anomic luxuries.

A post-natal mind
cleaves less decoratively
than those nursing double Ds.

Rub eucalyptus bottom balm
on a torn private sphere.

Suddenly trapped in a cloistered woman's
novel. Titled *All About My Stuff.*

How the material got physical.

It's not about not real just less fake.

Like babies, their mothers may
only see small pieces. Close-ups.
An exquisite corpse. Meaning:
the figure won't cohere. Only
toes, hands. No body
we understand.

Baby says, "Circles go
on top of each other."

All work is women's work.

That's bottom line balm.

A baby drinks Baby's Only.
A cow or a goat made it. You'll love it!
We want another drink
with some proof.
We are not unified,
not stacking toys.
How the material gets physical.
How we forget how to know.

TMZ

Another dead teen star; fluorescent
flowers wrapped in paper.

Figures of urban scandal, sundry
dis-appointees. A son's

suicide by leash. Song-
bird's questionable

incisors. Gender?
Lupine. She's putting "phony"

back into "phonetic."
We've invented osteo-parodic

abbrevs. We've forgotten
calm, masterful, time.

A star imports
craggy rocks for his drive-

way, completes his stalking
soundtrack. His girlfriend rocks

a hobo—bag not person.
No better fiction this year.

DEGREES

This town is a proverb: a woman
waiting. Thoughts have citations,
skies are marine.
All this strong weather.
Chance is dead or
just got tenure.
Mt. Olympus is a tea.
Fleeced heads loll on
valedictory brick. Jam jar
gaslights hold not much new.

Nobody's money made strangely.
No fragrant extras of our wilder port
cities: cleavage, pulse points,
direction. No secular vespers or seared
artichokes. No agented lust.
Read the town best in a porcelain
serving dish; the chipped tail
of its hand-painted fish.

INFINITE PROFILES

There's the blonde lonely post-grad.
Ephemeral one with plum-
colored nails, narrow feet.
She's Southern, tight,
a dater of art curators.
The other one is big-hipped,
a lost flower, singed before
he scrolled over to the overbite,
then to the Ivy-covered
hut. Afterwards he liased
with the super-professional.
Then the grave mother;
the rapscallion; a lady lugging
the abuse narrative. Then hung
with the sexpot. The Girl
of Recovery. Or was it lack?
Her ringlets, her kneeling chair
of lovelessness. And then the one
with the blessings of infertility.
A big-eyed network.

He knocked the youngest admin
up. All the paralegals knew.

And soon: his own instafamily.
An emergency adulthood blooming,
poppy of hardened red petroleum.
In his mind, the others now deleted.
In truth, they were still out there
in all his city's studios.

SELF SELL

Your ineffable Scotches,
half-classy, like an industrial
base-less hamlet. You're an ad
man picking apples on that hill,
marrying the image to the real.

That softer serve, that softer sell.
Spilling manners in eat-in alcoves.
Toddlers pretending paper
was money ignore us.

Aren't we all in on
the game? Called Ready
Or Not. Recommended
ages: zero to dead.
Number of players: infinite.

MEMENTO MORI

The 99 Cent Store
is a memoir. Stiff Levi
corduroys, crisping
paperbacks, plastic
tablecloths, votives.
Cappuccino also a dollar:
now-dead Italian owners
gestured chocolate.
NYC a furnace of art school
graduates worshipping garbage
cans. Even Jeff Koons'
patrons once were
dollar stores, as in
his sponge sculptures.

Our parents escaped the Bronx
for a more radically destroyed
place. "O Superman"
played while tubs clawed
the kitchen sink and asbestos-
rimmed windows.

At home, bad performance art:
outside, empty sidewalks,
that glass bottle glow.

Rachel, Saul, at 23 at parties
with the morose Israeli.
Theses unfinished,
thankful & unbuttoned.

Our breaks were cheap.
That is, already broken.
Before the self-harming
rent, strappy shoe
standalones, stores selling
amber scent. Readymades.
What art is made with a mop?
A religion of gutters.

The name of this piece is
My Life Has Already Happened.

DOWNLOADED

My auto-fill always writes
Dear Mom and Dad.
We are DVDs, cassettes, LPs,
even Betamax. Grandfather
liked offset type. It announced
the death of Ferdinand.
And these kids: content
managed, networked,
of their own devices.
For them, let's download Lit
about child murderers.
That is, children who murder,
while the elders recount
the Activism Age
as if telling Norse Sagas.
It seems the 1960s
were only good for
the people in them. A dream
of a better world helping
the dreamers more than
the dreamed of.
I am only trying to make
sense of what came later.

POEM FOR MAIA

A poem for Maia on her wedding day,
after Ted Berrigan's "Last Poem"

I have been reincarnated
while alive. Eartha Kitt purred,
"Cats have nine lives, you
have only one." Not for me.
Have been a scientist, producer,
author, and prisoner.
As the mug says
I love hugs and yet
as a child loathed to be
touched. Later I used
then surrendered to the power
they called higher
but only briefly as clichés
fail my probity.
I'm a secular devotee.
Of friends, mostly
but also a few difficult men.
I could sing their proverbial
harmonies. I went into debt

but then repaid; read
copiously; chatted on
Echo so much I got
carpal. I call and echo
in binary. Can you hear me
in the Twitterverse?
I fought those who coerced
the young in Utah,
trapping tattooed kids
in desert boot camps.
I declared myself Aspie.
My friends disagreed.
I had florid orange hair,
finally domesticated
by a curly salon maestro.
My heart throughout was perfect.

Perhaps my story has too much plot.
Most of all I like the sea;
it understands we
can reincarnate while
alive. I was reborn in
my fifth decade as a person
in love, a new devotee.
My happiest memories

are of the present (a paradox).
A kayak, a beaded dress for
dancing the Lindy.
Achieving the strangest
novelty of all,
consistency.

OUT OF POCKET

The memory of culture
is yet another culture.

Slang a shortcut
through history.

You wanted to be opiated,
to recover in a group.
Be prohibited to make
more desire.
In the crenelated black
shoe, blot of murky purple
lipstick, you tried to titrate.
Being a loser was the place
to be then. Restaurateurs hit on
you. Bosses tossed your dot
matrix resume. A thousand
Silk Cuts; the Bleckners
sold at auction an embossed
contagion. A "Mass Trick"
Treaty, a recession
of day laborers.

Today, girls iron
their hair. Obtaining
info without struggle.
"What's in your shopping
cart?" is a sample question.
Urban Dictionary informs
that "cunt" is over.
"Lady parts," the girls say,
asserting junk.

"We're girls," a young
one says. "We never
want to go to sleep."
I light a lamp, gesturing
at middle age as it enters
through the pores.
Longing for a lifelike
past. A step
to our disappearance.

Beware: memory's
an undiagnosed condition.
It costs. It's what we call
out of pocket.

CHANNELING

Overnight, binging turned positive.
Why does this water taste chemical?
A new filter is always needed.

We toss mizuna. You tell me authors
of the past believed in the Devil.
Is it so wrong to have diabolical
nostalgia? When that author is all
over speaker videos, handless mics,
gel lights, 17,000 Likes?

Remember the unheard. Dialect
indeterminate: a man hammering
cans into doors, a woman trading

little for little in a truly local market.
Let's pan then cut between these
stories. To avoid criticism, we'll use
different theme songs.

Those women at the spa have launched
a search for a holy leader.
But we have none over here,
only channels.

CURATORS OF CHAOS

Chalk marks on sidewalks
by children or for the murdered.
New portraits, faces preserved
by Restylane, their foreheads
like touch screens. The stay-at-
home's selfie. Abrasion
turning dermabrasion.

Order and disorder coexisting.
Donor twins, sharing, only vaguely,
the same material.

The tempura Plantagenets
turned screen savers.
Eternity as singularity.
The coded warrior princes unite
with the toy ad's anti-princesses.
Their castle: a copyright settlement.

These faces, figures,
shiny and binary. Art Brut
Athena meet Medical Aesthetics.

Once rulers,
then personae.
Now Anonymous.

SINKING IT ALL INTO

They were afraid.
Subtraction was
their favorite term.

If we were *arriviste*
we'd have arrived all ready.

Securities speak.
They say, "Take comfort."

Money cancels criticism.

If she were a he she'd be
indignant by now.

Her role, at this time:
an internal continuous
improvement consultant.

With one additional purchase,
you would have purchase.
With ability to purchase
you would be talking by now.

PERSEPHONE

You were turned statue.
Blood fingers went marble
then branched. Arboreal manicure.

Undersea lord father grasping
pomegranate princess.
Obdurate dread.
Persephone the marble
said: protect the young!
Deanimate old men!
Stone trapped in harm: cool-
tombed; asp-coiled.

We could see our catastrophe
in the pictures, statues.
Drones capture all
yet vets' coffins are effaced
from our vastest database.
All hidden, all pointed to.
And their trace:
the young that are
always on the run.

LOWRIDER

For Jeff

After the hot spot of surplus
we are bodies again.
Caught on the gears
of ten years ago.
Forced by scarcity
to be younger while
ever aging.
Poverty's paraphrase.

At first, bad
bosses and their offices
entered us, our hair in our
faces, running air quote
fiestas, betrayed by
the trusts, forgotten
by second wavers, their tears
for their own stalemate only.
With foundering Lib
we turned creatures
of code, of lowriders, footers,

template nothings.
Garbage: our poetic
resource. Coining words,
now for savings. Or something
that should be saved.

ACKNOWLEDGMENTS

The poems "Protocol," "Driftwood," and "Solarized" appeared in *The London Review of Books*. "The 51st State" has appeared in *Day One*. "Thief" appeared in *Jewish Quarterly*. "Views," "Instrumental," and "Degrees" have appeared in *The Awl*. "Spring Breaks," "My Own Private Idaho," "Holiday," "Lowrider," and "The Terms" appeared in *Open City*. "Red Riding Trilogy" and "Strip" appeared in *Fence*. "Green Fairy" appeared in *Feminist Studies*. "Express" and "Magnetic Resonance" were published in *Hanging Loose*. Other poems have appeared in *The Hat* and in *Solarized*, a chapbook published by Harry Tankoos Books.

I'd like to thank Keith Tuma for his thoughtful, careful edits and his support of this book. I'd also like to thank Amy Toland and the rest of the Miami University Press team. In addition, I'd like to express immense gratitude to Michael Scharf. His critical mind and many years of poetical support made this book possible. Thanks to Jorie Graham, Susan Howe and Steve Burt for their editorial suggestions. I am grateful to Siddhartha Lokanandi for all of his efforts to assist with this book. Special thanks go to Katy Lederer, Katie Degentesh, and Drew Gardner for sharp eyes. Shout outs for Lisa Dierbeck, Devorah Baum, Thomas Beller, Nuar Alsadir, Celina Su, Stephen O'Connor, Juliana Spahr, Zephyr Teachout, Ashwini Tambe, Susan Daitch, Joanna Klink, Christina Davis, Ann Peters, Tan Lin, Dale Maharidge, Eliza Griswold, Nathaniel Wice, Kevin Killian, Mark Bibbins, Daniel Soar, Jen Wolfe, Jim Lewis, Matthew Miller and Laura Secor for generously helping with, publishing, or reading pieces of this work at different junctures. Thanks to Jeff Clark, Tanya Selvaratnam, Rachel Urkowitz, Julie Lasky, and Anne Kornhauser. Special thanks to Marilyn Minter for permission to use her photograph *Spyder* (2005) as the basis for the cover of *Monetized*, and to Michelle Matson for assistance. Thanks to my beloved three-year-old daughter Cleo, who now has me transcribe her poetry. Finally, thanks to Peter Maass, for being a partner in all things and for his unswerving faith that I should write poetry.

Alissa Quart's poetry has appeared in the *London Review of Books*, *The Awl*, *Fence*, *Open City*, *Feminist Studies*, and many other publications, as well as in her poetry chapbook *Solarized*. She is the author of three non-fiction books: *Branded* (Basic Books, 2003), *Hothouse Kids* (Penguin Press, 2006), and *Republic of Outsiders: The Power of Amateurs, Dreamers and Rebels* (The New Press, 2013). Her nonfiction titles have been translated into 14 languages. She has written features for *The New York Times Magazine*, *Elle*, *The Atlantic*, *The Nation*, and many other magazines and has contributed frequent reported opinion pieces to *The New York Times* and elsewhere. With Barbara Ehrenreich, she is editor of the Economic Hardship Reporting Project, a non-profit that supports journalism about inequality. She wrote and produced the Emmy-nominated multimedia project "The Last Clinic" for *The Atavist*. She has taught at Columbia University's Graduate School of Journalism among other universities and was a 2010 Nieman Fellow at Harvard University.